First
riding lessons

WRITTEN BY
Sandy Ransford

PHOTOGRAPHED BY
Bob Langrish

KING*f*ISHER

Kingfisher would like to thank The Talland School of Equitation, Gloucestershire, England, and Hartpury College, Gloucestershire, England, for their invaluable help in the production of this book.

Kingfisher

Kingfisher Publications Plc
New Penderel House
283–288 High Holborn
London WC1V 7HZ

www.kingfisherpub.com

First published by
Kingfisher Publications Plc 2002

10 9 8 7 6 5 4 3 2 1

ITR/0502/TWP/CLSN(CLSN)/150SMA

A CIP catalogue record for this book is available from the British Library.

ISBN 0 7534 0692 6

Designed and edited by BOOKWORK

Editor: Annabel Blackledge
Art Director: Jill Plank
Designer: Kate Mullins

Consultant: Nikki Herbert BHSI

For Kingfisher:
Managing Editor: Miranda Smith
Managing Art Director: Mike Davis

Printed in Singapore

Contents

Before you start

Have you ever watched riders at a horse show, or simply practising in a field, and wished you were there riding with them? You could be. Anyone can learn to ride. You just need lessons.

Taking part in events

You may wish to take part in events – in showing, dressage, hunter trials or gymkhanas. If you ride well enough, you may not need to own a pony to compete. You might be able to borrow one, or even be asked to ride for someone else.

Why have riding lessons?

You may be told that, given a quiet pony to practise on, you can learn to ride on your own. Up to a point, this is true. You may learn how to make the pony move forwards, turn and stop. But compare these simple efforts with the style of a top dressage rider, or with the boldness of an eventer, galloping across country. Whether this is your dream, or whether you just want to ride for fun, taking proper lessons will be your first step on the road to success as a rider.

Hacking out with friends

Going for a hack in the countryside with your friends is one of the most enjoyable riding activities. You can explore new places, and you may spot all kinds of interesting wildlife, because animals are not afraid of horses. Your ponies, too, will enjoy being ridden out in the company of others.

Riding holidays

A riding holiday may mean pony trekking in Scotland, riding the range like a cowboy in the USA, exploring the mountains of Spain or having intensive lessons with a professional. You will have a wonderful time on a riding holiday, and you will enjoy it all the more if you are a good rider.

Where to have riding lessons

I t is important to choose a good riding school when you decide to have lessons. Look for those that are approved by an equestrian organization. Try to visit several schools, and check what facilities they provide. They should be orderly, and have a calm atmosphere.

Friendly instructors

The instructors at a good riding school will be friendly and helpful, even if they may sometimes be quite firm with you! You should be able to ask them questions and, if necessary, talk over with them any difficulties you may have. When they are taking classes, the instructors will wear boots and riding hats. They should also wear gloves when they are leading a horse or pony.

Happy horses

A row of clean, shiny heads looking out over their loose box doors, taking an interest in everything going on, is a good sign. The ponies must look well fed and their stables should be clean. The yard on to which they look out should be swept and tidy.

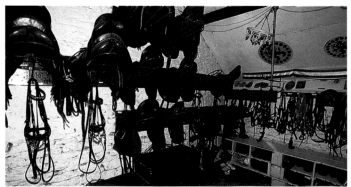

Tidy tack room

Tack must be clean and well cared for. There should be no cracked leather, fraying girths or stitching coming undone. Tack should be stored in a tidy tack room, which is heated in winter, with the saddles and bridles kept on brackets and hooks.

Lessons in the outdoor school

The riding school will probably have an outdoor school in which lessons are given. This is a fenced arena that may have a surface of bark or sand, kept raked smooth and level. Even if the school is just a fenced-off corner of a field, it should not be deep in mud.

Riding surface
The surface of an indoor school – sand, bark or synthetic granules – stays dry whatever the weather. It must be raked smooth.

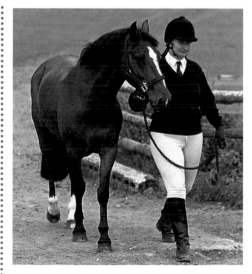

The indoor school

An indoor school, usually housed in a large barn, is a great asset to a riding school. Whatever the weather, you can keep dry for your lessons. And, in the winter months, it means you can ride in the late afternoons and evenings, when it is too dark to ride outside.

Watching lessons
Many indoor schools have an area where people can sit or stand to watch lessons in progress. If the indoor school is large enough, the riding school may hold competitions in it during the winter.

When work is over

In summer, at the end of a long day's lessons, the ponies may be turned out into the field to enjoy some well-earned freedom. In winter, they are likely to be stabled at night, and given feed and hay.

Clothes to wear for riding

Every sport has its correct clothing, and for riding this means a shirt and tie, a jacket, jodhpurs, boots, hat and gloves. Usually, the dress is more casual. The one essential item of clothing, on all occasions, is a hard hat.

Why wear riding gear?

Jodhpurs and boots are much more comfortable to wear for riding than jeans and shoes. Jodhpurs stop your legs being rubbed against the saddle; boots protect you from knocks from the stirrups.

Body protector

For any riding activity that involves jumping you should wear a body protector. It is a rigid waistcoat that protects your back in case you fall off.

Riding gloves with palm grips

Gloves

Riding gloves have special surfaces on their palms to help grip the reins. They may have leather or suede palms, or raised rubber pimples, which are useful in wet weather, when reins become very slippery. You should always wear gloves when you are riding, leading or lungeing horses and ponies.

Headgear

You must always wear a hard hat when riding. You should also wear it when you are leading or lungeing a horse or pony. Whether you choose a traditional hunting cap or a skull cap, you must make sure it is the right size. It should be fitted with a safety harness and comply with the latest safety standards.

A hunting cap has a rigid brim and is covered with fine velvet.

Casual clothes

For riding lessons, or going out on a hack, you will be comfortable in jodhpurs, boots, gloves, hat, and a shirt worn with a jumper or a jacket if the weather is cool.

Adjustable shoulder strap

A skull cap is a round, brimless helmet that is usually worn covered by a silk.

Safety harness

Silks with small brims are available in various colours to wear over skull caps.

Adjust the safety harness so that it is comfortable but holds the hat in place.

Skull cap and silk

Shirt and tie

Wool hacking jacket

Body-warmer under jacket

Western gear

Traditional Western riding gear means jeans, full-length chaps, fancy boots, a bandanna round the neck, a fringed jacket and a stetson. Many riders dress more casually. To protect their heads, today's young riders all wear hard hats.

Show gear
To compete in a show or other event you should wear formal riding clothes. You may wear a hacking jacket, or a black or navy show jacket.

Winter wear
A quilted, waterproof jacket is ideal for cold days, and half chaps help keep your legs warm. In wet weather a full-length mac will keep you dry.

Boots

There are two kinds of boots for riding: ankle-length leather jodhpur boots with elasticated sides, and full-length riding boots, which may be made of leather or a synthetic material. Long boots and half chaps, which you can wear with jodhpur boots, protect the inner sides of your legs from being pinched by the stirrup leathers. You can wear shoes when you are riding, but they must be strong and have a smooth, non-ridged sole and a heel.

Jodhpur boots protect your ankles.

Riding boots reach almost up to your knees and fit tightly.

Leather half chaps may fasten with straps or zips.

Measuring a pony

Traditionally, horses and ponies are measured in hands. One hand is equal to about 10cm, which is roughly the width of an adult's hand. Today, ponies are also measured in centimetres.

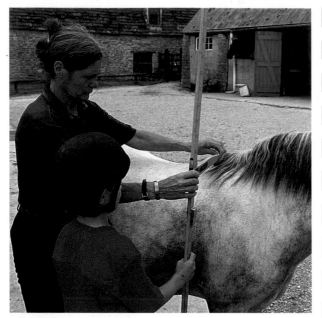

A measuring stick
An upright pole with a sliding bar enables you to read off the pony's height.

On the withers
The horizontal sliding bar rests on the highest point of the pony's withers.

Types of pony

Ponies may be a variety of shapes and sizes. They can be stocky and broad, so your legs can hardly reach round them, or they may be tall and narrow. They can be very hard work to keep moving, or go like the wind. For your first lessons you need a quiet pony. As your riding improves, you may graduate to a more lively one.

The right-sized pony

It is important that the pony you ride is the right size for you. If the pony is too large or too small, you will be unable to use your legs properly to give the correct aids, and you may find it more difficult to balance. If you are too large for the pony, you may also be too heavy for him to carry, and you could injure his back.

Too small a pony
This pony is too small for her rider. The rider's legs are too long to make proper contact with the pony's sides, and she may also be too heavy for the pony.

Too large a horse
This horse is much too large for his rider. The girl's legs do not reach far enough down his sides for her to be able to give the aids in the right place, behind the girth.

The right size
This pony and his rider are just the right size for each other. The soles of the rider's feet are level with the line of the pony's belly, so she can give the aids properly.

A variety of ponies

During your riding career you will meet many ponies. Physically, they will range from the hairy-heeled native type to the elegant, lightly-built thoroughbred type. Most will not be pure bred. Their temperaments will vary, too, from sluggish to highly excitable. Some ponies will need more experienced riders than others.

Half-bred pony
Half-bred means one of the pony's parents is a thoroughbred. This pony would suit a competent rider, and could carry out most activities.

Thoroughbred-type show pony
This kind of pony has beautiful paces, and goes well in the show ring. It would need an experienced rider.

Typical beginner's pony
A first pony might be a native breed, or cross-bred. It will be quiet and dependable.

Pure-bred native pony
A pony such as this Welsh Section A (Welsh Mountain) is an ideal all-rounder for a fairly experienced rider.

A pony's tack

Tack means the saddle, bridle and other equipment used on a horse or pony. Tack is usually made from leather, with stainless steel bits and stirrups.

Saddles and girths

Y ou need a saddle to give you a secure and comfortable seat on a horse's back. The girth holds the saddle in place. Saddles are made on a rigid frame called a tree. A canvas seat is stretched across the tree, and the padded seat goes over that. Saddles are made in different sizes and widths to fit differently sized horses.

A dressage saddle has straight flaps and a deep seat. It often has extended girth straps so that the buckles do not get in the way of the rider's leg contact with the horse.

Dressage saddle

A jumping saddle has forward-cut flaps and padding in front of the rider's knees (knee rolls), and behind their thighs (thigh rolls), to help keep their legs in the right position when jumping.

Jumping saddle

Types of saddle

Saddles are made in different styles according to the use for which they are intended. Mostly you will use some kind of general purpose saddle, but if you go on to take part in equestrian sports you may need to use a special saddle.

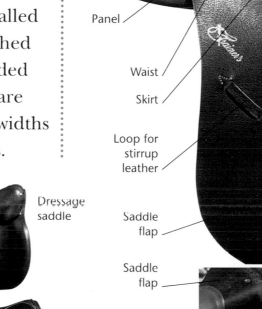

Cantle

Seat — Pommel — Gullet

D-ring

Panel

Waist

Skirt

Loop for stirrup leather

Saddle flap

Saddle flap

Girth straps

Buckle guard

A general purpose saddle has moderately forward-cut flaps and slight padding in front of the rider's knees. It is comfortable and suitable for most riding activities.

Types of girth

Girths may be made from leather, webbing, or synthetic fibres. Webbing girths were traditionally used in pairs. Leather girths, which may be made from a folded piece of leather or shaped like the Balding girth to avoid pinching near the horse's elbows, are expensive, but last a long time. String girths are cheap, but can pinch the horse's skin. Padded synthetic girths are comfortable and easy to maintain. For safety, girths should be fastened on either the front two, or the front and back, girth straps.

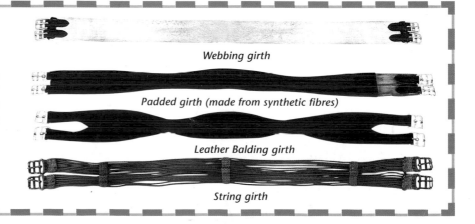

Webbing girth

Padded girth (made from synthetic fibres)

Leather Balding girth

String girth

Headcollars

Headcollars are put on horses' or ponies' heads to lead them and to tie them up. They may be made of webbing or leather. People tend to use webbing headcollars in the stable, and keep leather ones for special occasions.

The lead rope clips to the ring under the pony's chin.

Bridles and bits

A bridle and bit are the means by which a horse or pony is controlled by his rider. Bridles are traditionally made of leather, in three sizes: full size, cob and pony. Other materials are also used nowadays. There are two main types of bit – snaffle and curb – though there are many different varieties. Bits are usually made of stainless steel.

Snaffle bridle

A snaffle bridle, with a jointed snaffle bit and single reins, is the kind most often used. The headpiece buckles on to cheekpieces, which hold the bit in place. A separate headpiece is attached to the noseband, and fastens on the left.

Throatlash stops the bridle from slipping forwards

Cheekpiece holds the bit in place

Noseband

Stop, to keep the ring of a running martingale away from the bit

Eggbutt snaffle bit

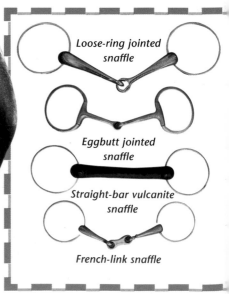

Loose-ring jointed snaffle

Eggbutt jointed snaffle

Straight-bar vulcanite snaffle

French-link snaffle

Browband Headpiece

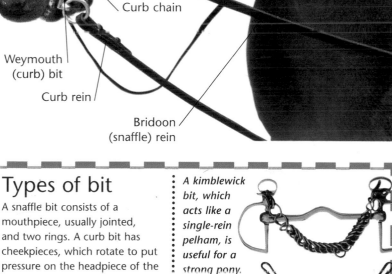

Bridoon cheekpiece

Curb chain

Weymouth (curb) bit

Curb rein

Bridoon (snaffle) rein

Double bridle

A double bridle has both a snaffle bit and a curb bit, and two pairs of reins. It is used only on well-schooled horses and ponies by experienced riders. The snaffle bit, or bridoon, raises the horse's head. The curb bit lowers the horse's head. The curb chain, tightening in the chin groove, gives extra control.

Roundings

Short leather straps that connect the curb and bridoon rings of a pelham bit, allowing single reins to be used with it, are called roundings. Their use means that the two functions of the bit cannot be separated, but some horses go well with them.

Running martingale

This attaches to the girth at one end. It passes through a neck strap, then divides into two straps that end in rings through which the reins pass.

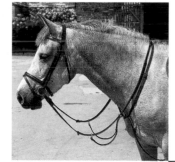

Standing martingale

Like a running martingale, this also attaches to the girth and passes through a neck strap, but the single strap is then fastened to the back of the noseband of the pony's bridle.

Martingales

Martingales are used to stop a horse carrying his head too high and evading the rider's control. They also prevent him throwing his head up in the air and possibly hitting the rider in the face. They should be fitted with care. They must not be so tight that they pull the horse's head down.

Types of bit

A snaffle bit consists of a mouthpiece, usually jointed, and two rings. A curb bit has cheekpieces, which rotate to put pressure on the headpiece of the bridle. It also has a curb chain, which presses on the curb groove and is held down by a lip-strap.

A kimblewick bit, which acts like a single-rein pelham, is useful for a strong pony.

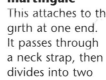

The two bits of a double bridle are the bridoon (snaffle) and Weymouth (curb).

A half-moon pelham combines the actions of the snaffle and curb bits. It would be used with a curb chain.

Tying a quick-release knot

When tying up a pony, fasten his rope to a loop of string, using a quick-release knot for untying in an emergency.

Loop the lead rope and put it through the string loop. Twist the rope a few times.

Make another loop in the end of the rope and push it through the first loop.

Tighten the knot by pulling on the headcollar end. Pull the free end to undo it.

Putting on a headcollar

You will need to put a headcollar on a pony in the stable so you can tie him up while you are grooming, tacking up and mucking out. You will also need to use a headcollar to catch him and lead him back from the field to the stable.

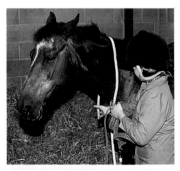

1 If the pony is outside, or if he is likely to wander around the loose box, first put the lead rope round his neck so you can hold on to him if you need to do so.

2 Put the noseband over his nose. Hold the cheekpiece of the headcollar in your left hand. Reach under his chin with your right hand to grasp the headpiece.

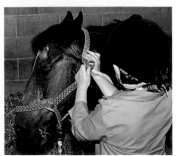

3 Bring the headpiece over the pony's head and fasten the buckle, tucking in the end of the strap. Tie up the pony using a quick-release knot.

Saddling up

When you have your first riding lessons, your pony will be already tacked up – that is, he will have his saddle and bridle on. But you will need to learn how to do this for yourself. Start by tying him up in the stable, then fetch his tack. You can hang the bridle on a hook or over the door while you saddle the pony.

Carry the bridle over your shoulder.

Carry the saddle over your arm with the pommel resting by your elbow.

Run the stirrups up the leathers.

Carry the girth over the saddle.

Carrying tack

To avoid trailing the reins on the ground, loop them up and put them with the bridle over your shoulder. Carry the saddle on your left arm, supporting it with your right hand. It is then in position for saddling the pony.

Putting on a saddle

The saddle sits just behind the pony's withers, and the girth goes round in the shallow groove just behind his forelegs. You put the saddle on from the pony's left side, but you must go round to the right side to fasten on the numnah and to check that the girth is correctly buckled on that side and not twisted.

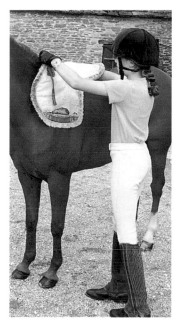

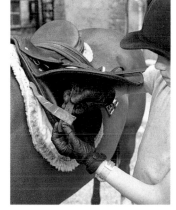

1 Hold the numnah in both hands, and lower it on to the pony's back, in front of where it will eventually go.

2 Put the saddle on top of the numnah, then slide them back together until they are in the right position.

3 Take the front girth strap out of the buckle guard and slide it through the loop on the numnah's strap.

4 Put the front girth strap back through the buckle guard. Repeat steps three and four on the left of the saddle.

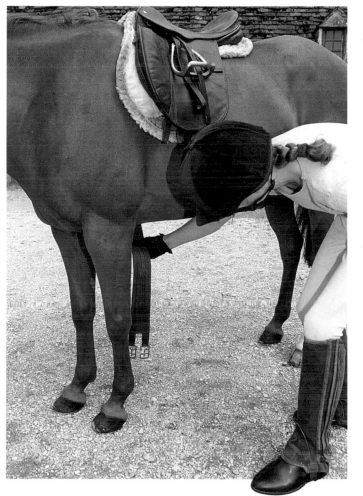

5 Let the girth hang down on the right side and check that it is not twisted.

6 Go back to the left side of the pony and reach underneath his belly to get hold of the end of the girth.

7 Fasten the girth buckles on the front two or the front and back girth straps. Smooth the skin under the girth.

Slide the guard back down over the girth buckles.

Putting on a bridle

A horse's or pony's head is very sensitive, so you must always handle it gently when putting on his bridle. Take care not to brush your arm or the bridle's cheekpieces against his eyes. Do not pull on his mouth when you put in the bit. If you do it slowly and methodically, putting on a bridle is not as difficult as it may appear.

How to put on a bridle

When you are learning, a bridle appears to be a very complicated piece of equipment. The key to being able to put it on without getting in a muddle is to hold it up by the headpiece and take a good look at it. The headpiece goes over the top of the pony's head, and the cheekpieces support the bit. The browband stops the headpiece slipping backwards, and the throatlash stops the bridle slipping forwards.

1 Carrying the bridle, approach the pony on his left side and undo his headcollar. Slip it off his head and then refasten the headpiece round his neck.

Checking the fit

A horse or pony usually wears the same bridle each time he is ridden, so it should fit him properly without much adjustment. But you need to know how the bridle should fit to be sure it is correct.

Before you put on the bridle, check that the noseband is level. If it is not, straighten it by easing its headpiece through the browband, pushing it up on one side and pulling it down on the other.

The cheekpieces should be buckled on to the bridle's headpiece at the same number hole on each side. If they are not, the bit will be pulled up more on one side than on the other.

When the noseband is fitted correctly, it should lie midway between the pony's cheekbone and his mouth. There should be enough room for you to slide two fingers between the noseband and the pony's nose.

When you have fastened the throatlash, there should be room for your whole hand to pass between it and the pony's cheek. If the throatlash is too tight it may interfere with the pony's breathing.

A snaffle bit should slightly wrinkle the corners of a pony's mouth when it is at the correct height. You can adjust the height of the bit by altering the length of the cheekpieces on each side of the bridle.

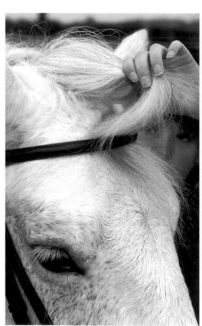

6 Pull out the pony's forelock from under the browband so it lies tidily over it. Smooth out any parts of the mane that are caught up in the headpiece.

2 Hold the bridle in your left hand by the headpiece. Take hold of the reins in your right hand and put them over the pony's neck.

3 Put your right arm under the pony's jaw and hold the bridle in your right hand. Holding the bit flat on your outstretched left hand, press it against the pony's lips.

4 If the pony does not want to open his mouth, wiggle your left thumb in the corner where he has no teeth. Press the bit against his lips as you do so.

5 When the bit is in the pony's mouth, put the bridle's headpiece over his ears, folding the ears down to enable you to do so.

7 On both sides of the bridle, check that the browband is not fitted so high up that it is pressing against the base of the pony's ears.

8 Reach under the pony's jaw to the right-hand side of the bridle for the throatlash. Check it is not twisted, then bring it round to the left side of the bridle and fasten the buckle.

9 Check that the bridle's noseband is not caught up on the cheekpieces, then fasten it behind the pony's jaw. Push the end of the noseband strap firmly through its keeper.

10 Do a final check on the bridle. Make sure the buckles are fastened properly and the ends of all the straps are in their keepers.

Saddle blanket

The horse wears a thick woollen blanket or pad under the saddle to protect her back from being rubbed. Traditionally, these blankets were hand-woven from sheep's wool, and doubled as bed-rolls.

Western tack

Western tack was designed for a cowboy's horse. The saddle was his home. It had to be comfortable, and to carry all his belongings, from bedding and food supplies to ropes and a rifle. The bridle had long reins. When they trailed on the ground, the horse was trained to stand still, as if tied up.

Western saddle

A traditional Western saddle weighs 18–22.5kg. Most modern saddles are lighter, but they all feature the horn at the front, to which steers were roped, and the high cantle at the back. The girth is called a cinch.

Horn Cantle

Flank strap

Skirt

Fender made of decorative leather

Seat jockey

Front rigging

Under the saddle flap
When you lift the saddle flap you can see the broad leather strap that carries the stirrup. The outer fender covers the strap and protects the rider's leg.

Wooden stirrup
The stirrup is made from a single, curved piece of wood. It is often covered with leather.

Putting on the saddle

If you are small, you may need help in carrying and putting on a Western saddle. It takes quite a lot of strength to lift it up on to a horse's back and settle it in place. You must never fling on the saddle, as you see in some films, because this would upset the horse.

1 First put on the saddle blanket, and then lower the saddle on to the horse's back.

2 Check the cinch is not twisted on the right side, then fasten it on the left side.

3 The cinch may be buckled or tied in place. Once you have fastened it, tuck in the free end of the leather.

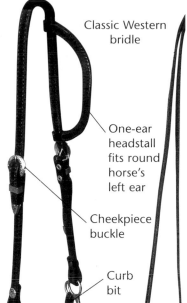

Classic Western bridle

One-ear headstall fits round horse's left ear

Cheekpiece buckle

Curb bit

Types of Western bridle

Instead of a browband, most Western bridles have a loop that fits round one of the ears to stop the headpiece slipping. For a trained horse, the bridle is usually fitted with a curb bit with a port (the half-moon shape in the centre). A hackamore controls the horse without a bit.

Putting on the bridle
With the bridle in your right hand and your right arm under the horse's jaw, press the bit into her mouth with your left hand.

Western hackamore
A hackamore is a type of bitless bridle. It uses a heavy, plaited rawhide noseband, called a bosal, to control the horse.

Reins

Seat of saddle

Horn

Headstall

Western bridles seldom have a noseband when the bridle has a bit

Long-cheeked curb bit

Saddle strings tie the rider's belongings on to the saddle

Cinch is made from woven hair or cord

All tacked up

The horse is now ready to be ridden. She is wearing a lightweight, modern Western saddle over a colourful saddle blanket. The long reins, which do not fasten together, are looped over the horse's neck to stop them from trailing on the ground.

First lessons

The first time you sit on a pony you will probably feel a little strange. As you have more lessons you will begin to feel at home on his back. Your first pony will be a very quiet one, and he will help your instructor to take care of you.

Greeting a new friend

When you meet a strange pony, walk up to him confidently. Hold out the back of your hand with your fingers curled into your palm, and let him sniff at it. Speak to him, and give him a pat on the neck.

Meeting your pony

When you go for your first riding lesson, your instructor will introduce you to the pony you are going to ride. It is a very exciting moment – although you may feel a bit nervous. If you do, try to hide it from the pony. Ponies quickly sense how someone is feeling and react to it. If you are anxious and upset, or worried, your pony will become anxious, too. If you act in a positive way, your pony will have confidence in you.

Getting ready
If you are having a group lesson, the ponies will be brought out into the stable yard for their riders to mount. Before you mount, you or your instructor should check the pony's tack. Your instructor will probably help you mount by holding the pony.

Setting off
When all the riders have mounted their ponies, and checked their girths and the length of their stirrups (see pages 30–31), the ride will leave the yard and set out for the outdoor or the indoor school.

Your first lessons

You may have individual riding lessons, or lessons with a group of other beginners. Either way, your instructor, or an assistant, will probably lead your pony with a leading rein. This clips on to the pony's bit rings, leaving you to hold the bridle's reins.

Getting to know a pony

Before you can handle and ride ponies, you need to know a bit about them. Ponies are gentle, nervous animals, happiest in a group. If something frightens them, their instinct is to run away. Living naturally, in a herd, they follow a dominant pony. When we domesticate them, we take that animal's place, and once they trust us, they will do as we wish.

Approach with confidence

When you approach a pony, talk to him in a friendly way. Give him a pat on the neck or a titbit, and handle him quietly and firmly. He will then feel confident. If you are nervous, hesitant or bullying, he will be upset and may behave badly.

How to lead a pony correctly

You lead a pony on his left side. Hold the lead rope or reins in your right hand up by the pony's head, and take the other end in your left hand. Walk forwards in a positive way beside the pony's shoulder without looking back at him.

Tips for handling horses and ponies

Speak to a horse or pony in a calm and friendly way as you approach him.

Approach towards his shoulder, from the front, where he can see you.

Never shout, rush about or make sudden movements near horses or ponies.

Be gentle but firm when you are handling horses and ponies.

Try to follow the same routine around the stable and with the horse each day.

Natural behaviour

Wild ponies live together in herds. If you turn a pony out in a field, he will immediately gallop off to join the others. If one pony shies at an object, the others will copy him.

Nervous or naughty?

A pony that hesitates about passing an unusual object may be frightened, or may be playing you up. Give him the benefit of the doubt and let him have a good look at it. Then drive him firmly forwards with your seat and legs, keeping on the pressure until he has gone past the object.

Gaining control

Once the pony walks past the object, relax your aids, and make a fuss of him. Pat him on the neck and tell him he is a good boy. If he refuses to pass the object, take him round in a circle and approach it again, reinforcing your aids with a whip if necessary.

Mounting block

A mounting block gives you extra height and stops you pulling the saddle over.

Hold the reins in your left hand and put your left foot in the stirrup. Spring off your right foot, with your right hand holding the saddle.

Swing your right leg over the horse's back and lower yourself into the saddle. Put your right foot in the stirrup, then take up the right rein.

Getting a leg up

Hold the reins in your left hand and put your right hand on the saddle. Your helper holds your left leg.

With your helper supporting your left leg below the knee, decide when he or she will lift, such as on the count of three. Lift yourself with your arms while your helper propels you up.

When you reach the level of the saddle, swing your right leg over it and sit down. Straighten your back, put both your feet in the stirrups, then take up the reins in both hands.

Mounting

Mounting means getting on a horse or pony. Although you may have help at first, you will need to manage alone. When you are out riding, you may have to dismount to open a gate, for example, and you must be able to get back on again. If you find mounting difficult because you are not very athletic and lack spring, or because you are not very tall, try letting the stirrup leather down a hole or two.

How to mount

There are various ways of mounting a pony. You may be able to use a mounting block or to get a leg up in the riding school, but you will also be taught the correct way to mount. When you are learning, you should have a helper to hold your pony. When you are on your own, you can stop him from walking forwards by standing him to face a wall or gate.

1 Stand on the pony's left side facing his tail. Hold the reins in your left hand. With your right hand, turn the stirrup towards you, and put your left foot in it.

2 With your left hand resting on the pony's withers, grasp the waist of the saddle with your right hand and at the same time spring up off your right foot.

Turning the stirrup

It is important that the stirrup iron and leather are turned the right way when you are riding. If they are not, the edge of the stirrup leather presses into your leg. This is not only very uncomfortable, it prevents you from using your legs properly.

Before you mount, turn the back of the stirrup iron towards you. As you mount and twist your leg and foot round, the stirrup turns so it ends up facing the right way.

To put your right foot in the stirrup, turn the front of the iron outwards. You may do this with your hand at first, but with practice you will be able to use your foot.

Western style

Start by facing the horse's left side. Hold the reins in your left hand, resting on the horn of the saddle. Put your left foot in the stirrup and your right hand on the back of the saddle. Spring up off your right foot. Swing your right leg over, taking care not to catch it on the high cantle. Lower yourself gently into the saddle. Put your right foot in the stirrup and take the reins in your right hand.

3 Swing your right leg up and over the pony's back, taking care you do not kick him with your toe as you do so. It is helpful if someone leans on your right stirrup as you mount to stop you from pulling the saddle over to the left when all your weight is on that side.

4 As you bring your right leg over the saddle, slide your right hand out of the way. Lower yourself down gently, do not flop.

5 Slip your right foot into the right stirrup, pointing your toe inwards as you do so. Take up the reins in both your hands.

Dismounting

The method of dismounting that starts with both feet out of the stirrups involves a certain amount of gymnastics. Most people consider it is the best way to get off a horse because it is the safest. The most dangerous thing that can happen to a rider is to be dragged along the ground by a moving horse because one foot is stuck in a stirrup. By taking both feet out of the stirrups and then jumping clear, you land on both feet together, and can walk on with the horse.

1 Hold the reins in your left hand and put your right hand on the pommel. Then take your right foot out of the stirrup.

Alternative way

An alternative method is to take your right foot out of the stirrup first, then vault off to land on both feet together. Unless the pony is trained to stand, you should get someone to hold him while you dismount this way.

How to dismount

When dismounting, you vault off the pony in one easy movement, so you have both feet on the ground very quickly and can walk beside the pony if he moves. As you land beside the pony, be careful to keep your own feet out of the way of his front hooves so he does not tread on you. Before you dismount, check that you are not going to land on uneven ground and risk hurting your feet or ankles as they take your weight.

1 Bring the pony up to a good square halt (see page 36) on a level piece of ground. If you think he may walk forwards, face a gate. Still keeping hold of the reins in both hands, take both feet out of the stirrups.

2 Pass the reins, and whip if you are using one, to your left hand. Rest them on the base of the pony's neck, just in front of the withers.

2 Swing your right leg over the pony's back and put your right hand on the waist of the saddle. Take your left foot out of the stirrup and vault off.

3 Slip to the ground, landing on both feet and bending your knees slightly as you do so. Then, with your right hand, take hold of the reins by the bit so you can lead him.

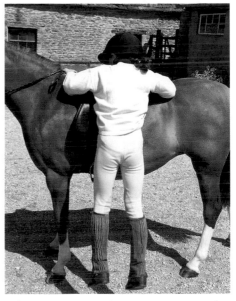

3 While still keeping hold of the reins in your left hand, put your right hand on the pommel of the saddle and lean forwards.

4 Swing your right leg up and bring it over the pony's back, taking care that you do not kick him as you do so.

5 Slip to the ground, landing lightly on both feet and bending your knees. Take hold of the reins near the bit in your right hand.

How to sit in the saddle

When you sit on a horse or a pony you should be relaxed and comfortable, yet alert and ready for action. You should sit well down in the saddle, with your back straight and your thighs and lower legs in contact with the saddle and the pony. Your body should be supple enough to follow all his movements.

How to hold the reins

Hold your hands in a relaxed position in front of you with the thumbs uppermost and the palms of your hands facing each other. Then take up the reins. Single reins should pass between your third and fourth fingers, up through your hands, and between your thumbs and first fingers.

Diagonal line

When you are sitting on the pony your arms must be in the right position. If you are holding the reins correctly, the reins and the lower parts of your arms should form a straight, diagonal line running directly from the pony's bit back to your elbows.

Foot position in stirrup

When you are putting your foot in the stirrup, turn the front edge of the iron outwards. Rest the ball of your foot on the stirrup iron and keep your toes pointing forwards and your heels pressed down.

Shortening reins

Hold both reins in your right hand while you slide your left hand down to the length you want. Then hold both reins in your left hand and slide your right hand down to shorten the right rein to the correct length.

Stirrup length

If you sit in the saddle and let your legs hang down naturally, the stirrups will be approximately the correct length when the treads of the irons are level with the insteps of your feet. You may need them a couple of holes shorter than this to start with, and when jumping.

Keep your head up and look straight ahead between the pony's ears.

Sit up straight, but do not hold your back stiffly.

Keep your upper arms relaxed and hold them close to your body.

Keep your seat in contact with the saddle and do not lean back.

Keep your heels down and your toes up.

Vertical line

When you are sitting in the saddle, imagine a straight vertical line running down beside you. If you are sitting in the correct position, the line would start at your ear and pass down through your shoulder and hip, before eventually finishing at the level of your heel.

Checking the girth

You should check the girth before you mount, but it is a good idea to check it again after a few minutes' riding. Some ponies blow themselves out when they are saddled and their girths are being tightened. Later, when they have relaxed, the girth may be too loose. You can adjust it from either side.

Keeping hold of the reins, lean forwards to slide your fingers under the girth. If you can get more than two fingers between the girth and the pony, then you need to tighten the girth.

Put your left leg forwards, lift the saddle flap and pull up the girth straps one at a time to tighten them.

Adjusting the stirrup length

You can adjust your stirrups when in the saddle, keeping your feet in them as you do so. With a bit of practice, you can do this by feel alone, without looking down.

Holding the reins in one hand, pull up the end of the leather with the other.

Undo the buckle, slide it to the correct position and put the prong in the hole.

Pull down the underneath part of the leather to slide the buckle up again.

The aids

Hand position
Keep your fingers closed while you keep an even contact with the horse's mouth.

The aids are the signals by which a rider communicates his or her wishes to a horse or pony. The aids are divided into natural aids – the rider's legs, hands, seat and voice – and artificial aids – whips and spurs. A well-trained horse responds to the lightest of aids, but a first pony may need stronger ones.

Boot with spur fitted

Spurs are attached to riding boots with leather straps.

Artificial aids

There are various kinds of whip. Long whips are used for dressage and schooling; short whips for ordinary riding; and canes, which may be leather-covered, for showing. Both whips and spurs are used to reinforce leg aids, although spurs should be used only by experienced riders.

Schooling whip

Riding whip

Riding whip

Hand position
Let your fingers relax and keep a loose hold on the reins.

Riding on a loose rein

At the end of a ride, and at intervals during a schooling period, it is a good idea to let the horse walk on a loose rein to stretch his neck muscles and relax. When you are riding on a loose rein, you still need to keep your lower legs in contact with the horse's sides, but you can ease the pressure on the reins. However, you must always be ready to gather up the reins quickly if something startles the horse.

Medium walk

Maintain a feel on the horse's mouth through the reins. With your lower legs, squeeze his sides behind the girth to tell him to walk forwards.

Leg position
Keep your heels well down and your lower legs pressed into the horse's sides.

Driving forwards

Sometimes ponies dislike or are afraid of particular objects, and refuse to pass them. When this happens, keep a firm hold of the reins and use your legs really strongly to drive the pony forwards.

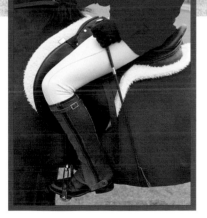

Using a whip

If the pony does not pay attention to your leg aid, you can reinforce it with a tap of the whip just behind the girth. A pony that behaves badly can also be given a sharp tap with the whip in the same place.

Expert rider

If you watch an expert rider performing a dressage test you will hardly notice any aids being given. The lightest of touches and slight shifts of weight in the saddle are enough to instruct the horse to carry out the most complicated movements.

A dressage rider rides with long stirrups. This is Nancy MacLachlan in 1998.

This dressage movement is called a piaffe. It is like trotting on the spot.

'Leg into hand' is the aim of riding. The legs drive the horse forwards; the hands control the energy created.

First-time rider

On the leading rein, the instructor has direct control of the pony. To help the rider feel safe on her first lesson, the instructor will tell her to hold on to the front of the saddle or a neck strap.

On the lunge or leading rein

Your first few riding lessons are likely to be on the lunge or on a leading rein. The instructor controls your pony, leaving you free to concentrate on sitting correctly and applying the aids. A lunge line is a long rein attached to a special headcollar, which the pony wears over his bridle.

Starting out
As the horse walks round in circles, the rider steadies herself by holding on to the front of the saddle.

Gaining confidence
Once the rider feels secure, she lets go of the saddle and holds the reins in the correct position.

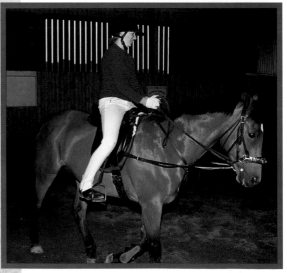

On the lunge

Riding on the lunge is a good way of learning to balance on the horse and to build up your confidence. It enables you to practise using the aids without having to worry about the horse's speed or direction.

Tips for first lessons

Get comfortable in the saddle before you start. Make sure that your stirrups feel right, and that the ends of the leathers are not sticking into your legs.

If you feel insecure, hold on to the front of the saddle, or to a neck strap.

Try to relax. Let your hands follow the movement of the pony's head.

Off balance

If you lose your balance when you are first learning to ride, it is tempting to try to hang on by pulling on the reins. You should never do so, however, as you can damage the pony's mouth and may make it very sore.

Trying too hard

When you first ride a horse or pony you must try to remember many things, but do not try so hard that you hold your body stiffly. Try to sit easily and let your body and hands follow the horse's movements.

Holding the reins
You can rest your hands on either side of the horse's withers to help you balance.

Headcollar
The horse may wear a headcollar to lead him by.

Using your legs
Squeeze with your legs behind the girth to keep the horse walking on.

Walking slowly
At first, the instructor will lead the horse round at a slow walk.

On your own

When you first ride off the lunge or leading rein, you will learn how to make your pony walk on and halt. This is not as easy as it sounds. The aim is to make the pony walk purposefully and with energy, and to halt when you tell him to do so. He should be balanced, alert and responsive to your aids at all times.

Square halt

To achieve a good, square halt, with the horse's forelegs and hind legs in line, you have to drive him forwards with your legs, then halt him with the reins. Although he is standing still, he should be full of contained energy, and ready to move off again.

Not listening

Some ponies ignore their rider's aids. Riders do not always give strong enough aids for their ponies, which then plod along sleepily with their noses stuck out. Applying the legs more strongly and shortening the reins will improve the pony's paces.

Keep a contact
Although you have stopped, keep your legs against the pony's sides and keep a feel on the reins.

Hind legs
A gentle nudge with your own leg will make the pony move his hind leg on that side into line.

Front legs
As you ride forwards into halt, try to make sure that the front legs are in line.

Working on the bit

When you are riding a horse or pony he should always be 'on the bit'. This means that his head is held vertically and his mouth is below the level of the rider's hands. In this position, the rider has the best possible control over the horse. It can be difficult to achieve and maintain, especially for an inexperienced rider and a pony that may not be perfectly schooled, but you can do it with practice.

Balanced
The pony is well balanced and ready to walk on again when you ask him to do so.

Head position
The pony is holding his head just behind the vertical, but he is striding out well.

Walk to halt, and halt to walk

This movement is achieved by pressure from your legs and on the reins. Although your lower legs, and your hands via the reins, should always be in contact with the pony, increasing or decreasing that contact tells him what you want him to do. Once he has obeyed your aids, you should relax them.

1 To ask a pony to walk on, put slight pressure on the reins and squeeze his sides with your lower legs behind the girth. As he obeys, relax the reins and the leg aid slightly.

3 Try to get the pony to halt squarely. Although you have stopped, do not completely relax your position. Maintain contact with your legs and hands to keep the pony alert.

2 To halt, increase the pressure with your legs, so driving the pony forwards into the bit. To stop him from moving forwards, resist the movement with your hands and the reins.

4 To move off into walk again, press your legs more firmly into the pony's sides and relax the reins a little to let him walk forwards. Then relax your aids, but maintain contact.

Turning left and right

When you are turning a pony, your outside leg and inside hand – that is, your right leg and left hand, if you are turning left – produce the movement. They are supported by the inside leg, which keeps the pony steady, and the outside hand, which reinforces the inside hand. The pony should not wander forwards while turning.

Your left hand moves back towards the pony's saddle.

View from above

When you look down on a pony and his rider as they turn, you can see how much the pony's body bends round the rider's inside leg. The rider's body shifts as it follows the pony's, and her head turns so that it faces the way she is going.

The left rein is pulled out to turn the pony's head.

Your right leg starts the movement with pressure behind the girth.

Your right hand is held close to the pony's neck.

The right rein supports the left rein by pressing against the neck.

The pony's bit is pulled to the left by the left rein.

1 Starting from halt, press your right leg into the pony's side behind the girth and feel your left rein.

Turning left

When you are turning left, the pony's forelegs and right hind leg move round his left hind leg. As soon as you have completed the turn, you should drive the pony forwards to walk or trot in a straight line.

2 Keep your left leg on the girth. Bring the right rein over to press on the pony's neck.

3 As he starts to turn, the pony's forelegs move in a semi-circle round his hind legs.

4 Continue to apply your hand and leg aids until you have turned the pony as far as you want to go.

1 Begin by pressing your left leg against the pony's side just behind the girth.

Turning right

In a turn to the right, the pony's forelegs and left hind leg move round his right hind leg. His neck and his spine bend in the direction of the movement.

2 Feel the right rein to turn the pony's head by bringing your hand out slightly.

3 Move your left hand towards the right to press the left rein against the pony's neck.

4 Continue to drive the pony round with your left leg. Try not to let him step forwards as he turns.

Practising rising to the trot

Before you learn to trot, practise rising with the horse standing still. Take your weight on your feet in the stirrups, stand for a moment, then sit down again. If you feel unsteady, rest your hands on the front of the saddle or on the horse's withers.

Stand up in the stirrups, keeping your knees slightly bent and taking your weight on the balls of your feet.

Lower yourself gently down to sit back in the saddle again. Do not let yourself flop down with a bump.

Learning to trot

The trot is a two-beat pace in which the pony's legs move in diagonal pairs: left fore and right hind, right fore and left hind. Because of this, it is very bumpy for the rider. To even out the bumps, you rise to the trot most of the time. But for more advanced riding, you also have to learn to sit to the trot. This is more difficult to do.

Rising trot

To rise to the trot you take your weight off the saddle by standing in the stirrups as one pair of the pony's legs moves forwards. Then sit down again as the opposite pair of legs moves. Try not to rise too high. At first, it is difficult to get the rhythm right.

Changing the diagonal

When you rise to the trot you are said to be riding on either the right or the left diagonal, according to which pair of the pony's feet touches the ground as you sit in the saddle. To change the diagonal, you simply sit for an extra beat and then continue rising again. You should change the diagonal when you change the rein (see page 49), and every so often when out hacking.

On the left diagonal the rider sits in the saddle as the pony's left forefoot and right hind foot hit the ground. Most people ride on the left diagonal when they are trotting a circle to the right.

On the right diagonal the rider sits in the saddle as the pony's right forefoot and left hind foot hit the ground. Most people ride on the right diagonal when they are trotting a circle to the left.

Sitting trot

To sit to the trot, you must keep your bottom and your thighs in contact with the saddle all the time and not bump about. You need good balance to do this, and you must relax the lower part of your back and allow it to absorb the pony's movements.

Transitions

A change of pace is called a transition. Going faster is an upward transition, going more slowly is a downward transition. To carry out transitions successfully you need impulsion, which is the energy you create in the pony by using the aids.

From walk . . .
Start with a good walk, with the pony striding forwards full of energy. To ask for trot, take a firmer contact on your reins and squeeze with your legs behind the girth. As the pony begins to move forwards into trot, ease your aids.

. . . to trot
As the pony starts to trot, relax your reins a little to allow him to move forwards, but maintain a contact. If he seems to want to go back to walk, you will need to re-apply your legs to keep him going. If necessary, use a whip.

Trot on
Once the pony gets into his stride you need to keep him trotting with a good, even rhythm. Keep a contact with your hands and legs. How strong this contact must be will depend on how forward-going the pony is.

From trot . . .
To carry out a downward transition from trot to walk, sit down in the saddle and squeeze with your legs behind the girth to drive the pony forwards into his bit. At the same time, resist the forward movement with your hands.

. . . back to walk
When the pony slows down to walk, relax your aids but still maintain contact with your legs and hands. You may still need to drive him forwards to get a good, free-striding walk, and you still need to maintain impulsion.

Canter on

The canter is a lovely pace once you have learned how to sit to it. At first you will bump out of the saddle, which is uncomfortable. To sit to the canter, you must keep in contact with the saddle, and at the same time try to relax.

The aids

To canter with the right leg leading, squeeze with your left leg behind the girth and feel your right rein. Keep your right leg pressed into the pony on the girth. Reverse the aids in order to canter with the left leg leading.

Keep your back straight.

Sit well down in the saddle.

Left leg gives aid for canter right.

Tips for cantering

Before you give the aids for canter, the pony must be going forwards well and be balanced. This will be in trot when you are learning. You must drive him forwards with your legs and control the energy with your hands, not let him trot faster and faster and become unbalanced.

Try to relax the lower part of your back when you canter, so you can follow the pony's movements.

Do not lean forwards out of the saddle, because the pony may interpret this as a signal to go faster.

Keep your reins fairly short and maintain contact with the pony's mouth so he cannot get his head down.

The pony should be light on his feet when he is cantering.

The gait

The canter is a three-beat pace, in which the horse's fore- and hind legs on one side are in advance of those on the other. The horse is said to be leading with, or on, the right or the left leg. When he is leading with the right leg, his feet hit the ground in the following sequence: left hind, right hind and left fore together, right fore. After this, there is a moment of suspension when all the feet are off the ground at the same time. A well-schooled horse can change the leading leg while in the air. This is called a flying change.

Good working canter

The working canter is the pace you will learn when you first start cantering. Travelling at average speed, the pony should move freely with a good rhythm, and respond to your aids at all times.

Keep a good contact on the reins so that you stay in control.

Keep the pony cantering with pressure from your right leg.

The pony's weight is on his left foreleg and right hind leg.

This pony is cantering with his right leg leading.

Checking leading leg

You should be able to feel which leg is leading in canter because the pony's shoulder on that side will be slightly in advance of his other shoulder. But when you are first learning, you may need to take a quick look down to check.

Ears laid back show that the pony is unhappy.

You are thrown off balance.

Your seat is thrown out of the saddle.

The right hind leg leads.

The left foreleg leads.

Right fore leading
The right hind and left fore are just hitting the ground.

Right fore leading
All the pony's weight is now taken on the right foreleg.

In the air
For a brief moment all the pony's legs are in the air.

Cantering disunited

When a pony leads with one front leg and the opposite hind leg in canter he is said to be cantering disunited. It is uncomfortable for both the pony and the rider. If it happens, go back to trot and give the aids for canter again.

Seat position
Sit down in the deepest part of the saddle, with your ear, shoulder, hip and heel aligning. Keep your heels down.

How to hold the reins
Separate the reins with your index finger and hold them above and in front of the saddle's horn.

Leg position
Ride with a nearly straight leg and a fairly long stirrup, letting your legs hang down lightly by the horse's sides.

Western riding

When riding Western-style you use only the lightest of touches to tell the horse what to do. When he has obeyed your aids and is carrying out your wishes, you sit still and do nothing. You do not need to keep in contact with his mouth, but hold the reins very lightly, except when giving specific aids. You use your voice as an aid to tell him to move forwards at different paces, and to halt.

Legs, seat and hands

You should sit up tall and straight in the saddle, yet be in a relaxed position. Rest the balls of your feet in the stirrups. You hold your hands higher than you would in English-style riding, at approximately the level of your elbows. When you are riding Western-style, you may hold the reins in one hand or two, except in competitions.

Turning left

Giving the aids for turning with the reins in one hand only is called neck-reining. The rein on the inside of the turn makes the horse look in the direction she is going. The rein on the outside puts pressure on her neck, telling her to move over.

1 Move your right hand to the left, so the left rein turns the horse's head in the correct direction and the right rein presses against her neck.

2 Look in the direction in which you want to go. At the same time, relax your left leg and push the horse over to the left with your right leg.

Turning right

When you are turning right, the right rein turns the horse's head to the right, and the left rein presses against her neck to tell her to move to the right. Your right leg relaxes and your left leg pushes the horse over.

1 The right rein starts the movement, and the left rein presses against the horse's neck.

2 Look towards the right and push the horse over with your left leg until the turn is completed.

Walk, jog, halt

Western riding is based on a system of ask and release. You ask the horse to move forwards or stop using your voice, reinforced by your legs and reins if necessary. As soon as he obeys, you relax the aids. This release is his reward. As the horse moves into a faster pace, his head will rise. As it does this, take up some of the slack in the reins, but do not pull on the horse's mouth.

Walk on
To ask a horse to walk forwards using Western-style aids, make a clucking noise. If he does not obey at first, make the noise again and tap his sides with both your legs.

Western jog
This is a kind of slow trot. Ask the horse for it with the clucking noise, reinforced with your leg aids if necessary, and shorten the reins slightly as the horse's head rises.

To halt
Push your weight down into your heels and brace your body, while saying, "Whoa." If the horse does not obey, raise your reins a little to put pressure on the bit. Repeat the rein aid if necessary.

In the school

When you have learned how to ride at the basic paces, and can control a pony on your own, you will progress to carrying out various exercises in the riding school. These will improve your skills and make you a better rider.

A group lesson in the school
In a group lesson, you have to keep up with the pace of the pony in front of you, and keep your pony's mind on his work.

Passing shoulder to shoulder

While you are riding in the school you may have to ride past another pony and rider. When you do this, you should pass left shoulder to left shoulder. This is also the generally accepted way of passing another rider you may meet when out hacking.

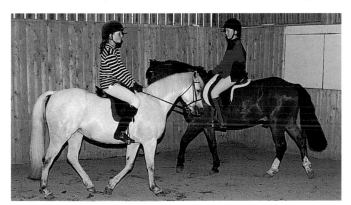

Riding at the correct distance

When you are riding in a group you must leave a pony's length between your pony and the pony in front of you. Riding close up behind another pony may upset it, and it might kick out at your own pony and injure it, or you.

Riding in a group

Riding in a group can be quite a challenge at first. There are many things to remember. You must control your own pony, but at the same time consider what other riders are doing. Your pony may behave differently, too, in the company of others. He may be more excitable, or he may refuse to leave the other ponies to carry out your wishes. You will learn both from your own riding, and from watching others.

Exercises in the school

C arrying out individual exercises in the riding school that involve changes of pace and direction, such as riding circles and loops, is a good way of testing your riding ability. You must manage your pony and give the correct aids at the right time. Your instructor will help you if you need advice.

Riding exercises in pairs

If you have four or more riders in your group you can carry out exercises in pairs. This is fun to do, but it is a great test of timing and judgment. You must keep level with each other all the time, which is difficult if one pony has a longer stride than the other. You might ride up the school, circle in opposite directions, then pair up again. With practice, you can do this at trot and canter.

Dressage arena

Most riding schools are marked out with letters like a dressage arena. You can use the letters as points at which to change your direction or pace. For example, you might walk from K to H, trot to F, and so on. To remember the sequence of the letters, use a phrase like 'All King Edward's Horses Can Make Big Fences'.

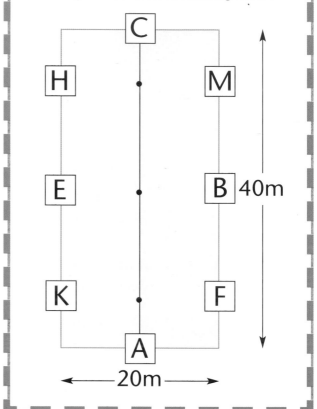

Changing pace

If you are told you must walk to H and then trot to M, you should break into a trot as your pony's shoulder becomes level with the letter. It is quite a challenge, and your pony must be well-balanced and obedient to your aids. You have to judge exactly the right moment to give the aids, and you must deliver them very precisely. This takes much practice.

Figures to ride

The top row of figures shows ways of changing the rein – that is, altering the direction in which you are riding round the school. Some of the other figures also involve a change of rein. The aim is to make all these shapes as accurate as possible. A circle should be round, not flattened. A figure-of-eight should be made up of two equal circles. The loops of a serpentine should also be of equal size.

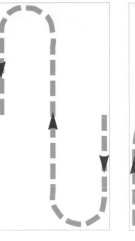

Ride up the centre from the right rein and then turn left to change the rein.

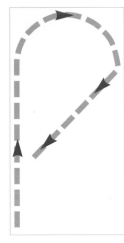

Ride across the centre of the school and then turn left to change the rein.

Ride across a short diagonal, such as from M to E, or from corner to corner.

Riding a two-loop serpentine across the centre is another way of changing the rein.

A 5-metre loop is a curve that goes up to 5 metres in from the long side of the school.

You can ride circles of 10 and 20 metres in diameter from a number of points.

Riding a figure-of-eight's two complete circles involves two changes of rein.

Riding a three-loop serpentine leaves you going in the same direction as you started.

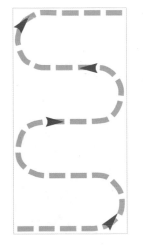

Riding a four-loop serpentine means you end up going round in the opposite direction.

Without stirrups and reins

O nce you have had a few riding lessons you may be asked to ride without stirrups, and, later, without reins. Riding without stirrups is an excellent way of improving your seat in the saddle. Riding without reins improves your balance. You should never rely on the reins to keep your balance.

Whole ride no stirrups

When you have riding lessons, you may spend part of each session riding without stirrups. To stop them banging against the pony's sides, you cross them over in front of the saddle. The ride may walk or trot round together, or you may take it in turns to trot round while the rest of the ride walks.

Lungeing without reins

When riding without reins you should tie them in a knot in front of the horse's withers to stop them hanging loose. When you are on a lunge rein, you do not have to worry about steering or stopping the horse, although you will learn to change direction using your legs.

Walk on the lunge
You can concentrate on your position in the saddle and use the leg aids to control the horse's pace and direction.

Trot on the lunge
You may feel insecure when trotting. If so, hold on to the front of the saddle or a neck strap with one or both hands.

Without stirrups

Let your legs hang down beside the pony. Keep them pressed against his sides, with your heels down and your toes up.

Try to sit deep down in the saddle and not bump out of it.

Relax your back so you can follow the pony's movements.

Riding without stirrups is hard work on your muscles, and your legs will ache afterwards.

Holding on to the saddle

When you first ride without stirrups, you will probably hold on to the front of the saddle with one hand while you hold the reins with the other. Your instructor may take you on a leading rein or on the lunge until you become more experienced.

The instructor will lead your pony very slowly at first to let you get used to being without stirrups.

Sit up straight, as if you had stirrups.

If you hold both reins in one hand, keep it in the correct position.

Without reins

Riding without reins is a test of balance. An experienced rider should be able to ride independently of the reins.

Using your leg aids, practise turning the pony right and left.

If you lose your balance, hold the saddle or neck strap.

If your pony misbehaves, or tries to run off, get hold of the reins immediately.

Trot on your own

When you have become more experienced at riding without stirrups you will be allowed to ride on your own. You can walk, trot, canter and even jump without stirrups. You will need to use both hands on the reins, though if you feel unsafe you could rest your hands, still holding the reins, on the front of the saddle. You must keep contact with the pony's mouth.

Forwards and backwards

Keep your seat in the saddle with your legs in the correct position. Then lean forwards to touch the horse's head behind his ears, or as far as you can reach. Go back to your starting position, and then lean backwards to touch the top of the horse's tail, twisting at the waist as you do so. Do not pull on the horse's mouth.

Round the world

In this exercise you go round in a complete circle while sitting on the horse. As you move round, steady yourself by holding on to the saddle.

Exercises in the saddle

Doing stretching and twisting exercises on your pony is good fun. They will help to make you supple, and once you have had a bit of practice doing them, you will become a more confident rider. Start all the exercises by sitting in the correct position in the saddle (see pages 30–31). Only practise the exercises when you have someone with you who can hold your pony.

1 Tie your reins in a knot on the horse's neck and take both your feet out of the stirrups.

2 Lift your right leg over the horse's neck, taking care not to kick him as you do so.

3 Swing your left leg over the quarters. Hold the saddle with your right hand.

4 You are now facing backwards. It feels very odd without the horse's neck in front.

5 Start going back by twisting round and swinging your right leg over the horse's back.

6 Hold on to the front and the back of the saddle as you sit on the horse facing sideways.

7 Shift yourself round in the saddle as you prepare to move your left leg back over again.

8 Swing your left leg back over the horse's neck to return to where you started.

Arm exercises

Stretch your arms high up in the air, then rest your hands on your shoulders. Stretch both your arms out to the sides, and bring your hands back to your shoulders. Reach forwards, and then go back again.

Leg stretching

Sit in the correct position in the saddle and keep the upper part of your legs still. Swing your left leg forwards as far as you can, moving it from the knee downwards. Then swing it back as far as you can. Repeat the exercise with your right leg. Now bring both legs back to the usual position. Moving one at a time, point your feet downwards as far as they will go, then upwards, to stretch your ankles.

Leaning back

You may need to hold on to the front of the saddle to do this exercise, but try to manage without doing so. Simply lean right back until your head is resting on the pony's quarters. Stay there for a moment or two, then sit up again. This is a good way of developing the strong stomach muscles you need for riding.

Touching toes

Lift your right hand up in the air, then bend down over the left side of your saddle and touch your left toe. Straighten up again, and repeat the exercise, lifting your left hand up and bending down to touch your right toe.

Your first jumping lessons

Approach
The approach to a jump is all-important. You must drive the pony firmly forwards with pressure from your legs.

Learning to jump is very exciting. There is much to learn, but if you ride correctly over trotting poles and small fences, in time big fences will not be a problem. The pony must be moving with impulsion before take-off, and you must follow his movement over the jump.

Forward position

For jumping or galloping you need to learn forward position. When jumping, shorten the stirrups a hole or two. Lift your bottom clear of the saddle and lean forwards, taking your weight on your knees and on your feet in the stirrups.

Leading over poles

First jumping lessons for both ponies and riders are usually over poles laid on the ground and spaced so the pony can walk and trot over them. To start with, your instructor may lead your pony over them.

The galloping position

You also use forward position when galloping to take the weight off the horse's back. Shorten your reins and keep your knees pressed into the saddle and your heels down. If your heels come up you will lose your balance.

1 As you approach the poles, shorten your reins slightly and go into forward position. Drive the pony on with your legs. Keep your heels down and your head up, and look ahead to where you are going.

2 The pony will lift up his feet to trot over the poles. He should move smoothly and evenly, with a regular rhythm, and not jump over the poles. Use rising trot when you are trotting over poles.

Keep your legs in contact with the pony's sides and your heels down during the jump. Feel the reins, but do not pull.

Take-off
When the pony's hind legs propel him into the air, lean forwards to go with his movement. Let your hands follow his head.

Trotting pole practice

Trotting over poles is a good exercise for a pony. Lay three or four poles 1 to 1.3m apart, according to the pony's size. When the spacing is correct, the pony's hind foot will hit the ground mid-way between two of the poles.

1 Walk over the poles at first. Go round the school and try approaching them from both directions. Use forward position as you ride over the poles.

2 When you are happy in walk, trot round the school and, as you go round, take in the row of poles. Keep a good rhythm in the trot, and look ahead as you ride, not at the poles.

Your first jump

After trotting poles, you will learn to take your first jump. It will not be very high. Crossed poles encourage the pony to jump in the centre, where the fence is lower. Wings placed at each side of a jump help to prevent the pony from avoiding it and running out. This counts as a refusal in competitions.

Landing
When the pony lands, keep the forward position and take care you do not pull on his mouth.

Sequence of a jump

A jump can be divided into four parts: the approach, the take-off, in the air and landing. You can approach a jump in trot or canter – both must be balanced and rhythmical. The take-off must be at the right distance if the horse is to clear the fence. Once he has landed, do not hesitate but ride him straight on towards the next fence.

Looking forwards

Once you have learned to ride you can enjoy many activities. You might join a pony club and go away to camp. You can hack out with friends, and take part in horse shows and gymkhanas.

Hand signals on the road

Give clear signals to pedestrians and cyclists as well as drivers, leaving plenty of time before you carry out your intended movement. Hold your reins firmly in the other hand to keep control of your pony.

Riding safely on the road

Always ride on the correct side of the road and keep to the inside. Never ride more than two abreast, and stick to single file on narrow lanes. If you are riding two abreast, then the rider on the inside of a turn to the left or right should make the hand signal.

Road safety

Before you ride out on the road, learn the systems of rules and signals that apply. If possible, take a road safety test. Make sure you can control your pony in all situations. Avoid riding on main roads and narrow roads that do not have grass verges. Never ride on the road at night or when it is foggy.

Turning right
When you wish to turn right, first check behind you that no vehicle is approaching. Hold your right arm out straight to give the signal. Check that it is safe to turn before you do so.

Turning left
To turn left, check for approaching vehicles, then hold your left arm out straight to give the signal. Before you make the turn, check again that it is safe for you to do so.

Thank you
To thank a driver who slows down for you, raise a hand and smile. If you do not wish to take a hand off the reins, nod your head and smile at the driver.

Stop
If you wish to ask another road-user to stop, hold up your right hand in front of you. Do not be afraid of asking drivers to stop or slow down if necessary.

Asking traffic to slow down
To ask a driver to slow down, hold your outside arm out to the side and move it slowly up and down. Thank them when they do slow down.

Light-reflective equipment

You should never ride on a road at night, but on gloomy winter afternoons you can wear light-reflecting safety gear. You can buy reflective belts, tabards and hat covers for yourself, as well as bridle covers, leg bands, tail guards and exercise sheets for your pony. You can also buy lights that clip to your stirrups, showing a white light at the front and red at the back.

Safety tabard
A safety tabard fits over your outdoor clothes. It may have a light-reflective strip across the back and front, or it may feature a warning to other road-users, such as 'Caution: horse and rider', or 'Please pass wide and slow.'

Reflective strip

Safety tabard

Riding out

Hacking – going out for a ride – with friends is fun. If you plan your route beforehand you can make the ride more interesting. You might explore woods and commons – taking in fallen logs as jumps – canter along a bridleway or even ford a shallow stream. Tell an adult where you are going and when you expect to return.

Riding across open ground

It is fun to have a canter or a gallop across open ground if you are allowed to do so, but make sure that you can control your pony before you start. Go uphill if possible, and keep at least a pony's length away from other horses.

Opening and closing gates

A gate on a bridleway should have a catch that you can reach when mounted. You should then be able to open the gate, walk through it and close it without dismounting. Practise at the stables before you try it out riding.

1 Ride right up to the gate and position your pony alongside it so you can reach out to work the catch.

2 Lean forwards to release the catch. Keep your pony standing still with the reins in your other hand.

3 Push the gate open and hold on to it while you ride through. Do not let it swing back on your pony.

4 Once through the gate, turn your pony round and close it again. Make sure the gate is securely shut.

Riding on bridleways

In some areas you may be able to use bridleways – tracks on which horses and ponies are allowed – for all or part of your ride. When riding on a bridleway, follow the signposts and do not stray from the track if it crosses a field. Look out for farm animals, and make sure that any gates you may go through are closed and properly secured.

Riding past other animals

You may ride past a field in which other horses, or cattle, charge about and upset your pony. Try to keep him calm. Keep your reins short and use your legs strongly to ride him past them.

Riding a pony through water

Only cross a stream if you know the water is shallow. Many ponies are nervous of water unless they know that there is firm ground beneath it. Let the pony take his time at first, but then drive him on firmly with your legs and seat.

Ready to move on

As your riding improves, you can progress. You might learn how to do dressage, or improve your jumping until you are good enough to enter competitions. If you enjoy galloping and jumping across country you might compete in hunter trials or eventing. Whatever your aim, you will need to work hard to achieve it.

Turn on the forehand

The pony turns through 180 degrees, with his hind legs and outside foreleg moving round the inside foreleg. To perform a turn on the forehand to the right, feel the right rein and keep the contact with the left rein. With your right leg behind the girth, push the pony's quarters round step by step. Keep your left leg in contact behind the girth throughout the turn.

Going faster

Only gallop when you are sure you can control your pony. If you are with other ponies and riders, spread out and leave plenty of space between you. Try to gallop uphill, because it is then much easier to stop. Go into forward position (see page 54), and keep your reins short.

Improving your riding skills

No matter how good a rider you are, there is always more to learn.

Try to ride a variety of ponies – they will teach you a lot.

Never forget the basic principles of riding and handling horses and ponies.

Competitive riding

You may be happy to spend your time hacking, but you might want to compete. Whatever kind of equestrian sport you wish to enter, your pony must be fit, well-schooled and obedient. Even if jumping is your aim, you will have to spend a lot of time doing flat work to prepare him for competitions.

Showjumping
You may aim to become a top-class showjumper, but you will have to start by entering novice competitions at local shows. Your pony must be a careful jumper, and you need to be able to plan your round and remember the course.

Cross-country
To succeed in eventing or hunter trials you must be a bold and confident rider. You need a fast pony with the stamina to keep on galloping, even though he may be tired, and the courage to tackle fences at speed.

Dressage competitions
Dressage is an extension of the work you do in the riding school. You need to work hard at perfecting the pony's paces and transitions, and you must be able to give very accurate aids. You can start competing at pony club level.

It may look easy, but both horse and rider are working very hard.

Mounted games
Gymkhanas and some horse shows hold all kinds of games and races in which you can compete either as part of a team or as an individual. You need to be good at games yourself, and have a fast pony that can turn quickly.

A small, agile pony is ideal in a gymkhana race.

If your pony does not obey you, ask yourself if you gave the aids clearly enough, and try again.

Whatever kind of riding you are doing, be decisive in your actions; do not hesitate.

When you are jumping, apart from going into forward position, try to keep still in the saddle.

Do not overface your pony, or work him so hard he gets stale. Take him hacking for a change.

Keep your hands still and relaxed, apart from when you are giving specific aids.

Glossary

Numnah

Mounting block

You may not understand all the words you come across as you read about horses and ponies, and get to know more about their world. This list explains what some of them mean.

action The way a horse or pony moves.

aids The signals that a rider uses to tell a horse what to do. Natural aids are the rider's legs, **seat**, **hands** and voice. Artificial aids include whips and spurs.

approach The last few **strides** a horse or pony takes before a jump.

balance A horse is balanced when his weight, and that of his rider, is distributed so that he can move easily and efficiently.

body protector A rigid waistcoat that helps to protect your back if you fall off a horse or pony.

bridleway A path or track on which horses and riders are allowed.

bridoon A **snaffle bit** used with a **double bridle**.

browband The part of a bridle that fits round a horse's or pony's forehead and stops the **headpiece** from slipping backwards.

cantle The back of a saddle.

changing the rein Changing the direction in which you are riding round the **school** or show ring.

chaps Leather or suede over-trousers worn to protect a rider's legs when riding.

cheekpiece The part of a bridle that supports the bit.

cheeks a) The flat sides of a horse's face. b) The vertical side parts of a **curb bit**.

cinch The **girth** on a Western saddle.

cob A short-legged, small, stocky horse, usually with a **quiet** temperament.

cob-sized Medium-sized – of a bridle or a headcollar.

collection Moving with shorter, more elevated strides, thus shortening the horse's or pony's **outline**.

contact The link through the **reins** between a horse's mouth and his rider's **hands**.

curb bit A bit with **cheeks** and a curb chain that acts on a horse's head and chin as well as his mouth.

diagonal a) A pair of the horse's legs diagonally opposite each other, e.g. left fore, right hind. b) A slanting line across a **school**.

disunited Cantering with one leg leading in front and the opposite leg behind.

double bridle A type of bridle with two bits.

dressage The advanced schooling and training of a horse, performed in competitions.

eventing A competition comprising **dressage**, cross-country and showjumping.

extension Moving with longer, lower **strides**, thus lengthening the horse's or pony's **outline**.

fender A leather flap that covers the stirrup leather on a Western saddle.

flat work The work a horse or pony does on the ground, as opposed to over fences.

flying change Changing the **leading leg** at canter when a horse has all four feet off the ground.

forehand The head, neck, shoulders, **withers** and forelegs of a horse or pony.

forelock The part of a horse's or pony's mane that falls over his forehead.

forward position Leaning forwards with the seat off the saddle, taking the weight on the knees and feet, used when galloping and jumping.

gait The **pace** at which a horse or pony moves. The natural gaits are walk, trot, canter and gallop.

girth The broad strap that goes round a horse's belly to hold the saddle in place.

gymkhana Mounted games and races, usually performed as part of a show.

hack a) To go out for a ride. b) A type of riding horse.

hackamore A type of bitless bridle that may be used in Western riding.

half-bred A horse or pony with one **thoroughbred** parent.

half chaps **Chaps** that extend from the ankle to just below the knee.

hands a) The units of measurement used for a horse's or pony's height. One hand equals 10cm. b) A rider who has light but positive control of the **reins** is said to have good hands.

headpiece The part of a bridle or headcollar that goes over the horse's head.

hunter trials Cross-country jumping competitions.

hunting cap A velvet-covered hard riding hat with a brim.

impulsion The energy a rider creates in a horse by the use of the legs and **seat**.

jodhpur boots Ankle boots worn with **jodhpurs**.

jodhpurs Riding trousers that have pads on the inside of the rider's knees.

jog a) A slow trot. b) A **pace** in Western riding.

keeper A small loop on a strap through which the end is put to keep it flat and tidy.

Skull cap

Measuring stick

Safety tabard

Take-off

Jodhpur boot

landing The stage of a jump when the horse's feet reach the ground again.

leading file The horse and rider at the front of a group.

leading leg The leg that is in advance of the others when a horse is cantering.

leg into hand A riding term meaning that you create energy in the horse or pony with your legs and control it with your hands.

leg up An easy way of mounting, in which a helper holds the rider's left leg and helps them to spring up into the saddle.

loose box A separate stable in which a horse or pony is free to move about.

loose rein When on a loose rein, the rider has no contact with the horse's mouth.

lungeing Exercising a horse on a long rein that is attached to a special headcollar.

martingale A piece of **tack** designed to stop a horse from throwing up his head too high. A standing martingale runs from the **noseband** to the **girth**; a running martingale from the **reins** to the girth.

measuring stick A scale from which you can read off a horse's height.

native pony A breed such as Exmoor, Welsh or Highland that was bred on the moors and mountains of Britain.

near side The left side of a horse or pony.

neck-reining A way of turning used in Western riding in which both reins are held in one hand.

noseband The part of a bridle that goes round a horse's or pony's nose.

numnah A saddle-shaped pad used under a saddle to prevent it from rubbing the horse's or pony's back.

off side The right side of a horse or pony.

on the bit A horse's head held in the position in which the rider has the maximum control of him.

outline The shape a horse's or pony's body makes when he is being ridden.

overface To ask a horse to do work, such as jumping, which is beyond his current stage of training.

pace a) Another word for **gait**. b) A gait in which a horse moves both legs on one side together.

pommel The front part of a saddle.

port A raised, half-moon shape in the mouthpiece of a **curb bit** that allows room for the horse's tongue.

quarters The parts of a horse or pony behind the saddle – his hindquarters and hind legs.

quiet Said of a calm horse that is not easily upset.

rein back Stepping backwards. The horse's legs move in **diagonal** pairs.

reins The parts of a bridle that run from the bit to the rider's hands.

rhythm The evenness and regularity of the horse's or pony's hoof beats.

running out When a horse or pony refuses to jump a fence by going round the side of it.

safety harness The adjustable straps that hold a riding hat in position.

safety tabard A vest worn over riding clothes to warn motorists of the rider's presence or that the horse is nervous.

school a) A riding arena. b) To exercise a horse for its education and training.

seat a) A rider's position in the saddle. b) The part of the saddle on which a rider sits.

silk A fabric cover for a **skull cap**, available in a range of colours.

skull cap A hard hat used for riding.

sluggish Said of a lazy pony that is reluctant to work.

snaffle bit A bit that is usually jointed in the centre and has two rings.

stride The distance travelled by a horse's foot between two successive impacts with the ground.

suspension The moment in canter when all the horse's feet are off the ground at the same time.

tack All the pieces of saddlery used on a riding horse or pony.

tack room A room in which tack is stored. It is fitted with racks for holding saddles, and bridle hooks.

take-off The stage of a jump when a horse launches himself into the air.

thoroughbred A breed of horse registered in the General Stud Book. All racehorses are registered thoroughbreds.

throatlash The part of a bridle that goes under the horse's throat and stops the bridle from slipping forwards.

transition The change from one **pace** to another. An upward transition is from a slower to a faster pace; a downward transition is from a faster to a slower pace.

trotting poles Poles laid on the ground for training a horse or rider to jump.

waist The narrowest part of a saddle's **seat**.

wings The sides of a jump.

withers The bony ridge at the base of a horse's neck.

working canter A pace between collected and medium canter.

Index

HORSE AND PONY WEB SITES
www.hartpury.ac.uk
(information on courses run and events held at the centre)
www.talland.net
(information about the school and the courses run there)
www.pony-club.org.uk
(official Pony Club web site)
www.bhs.org.uk
(official British Horse Society web site)
www.ilph.org
(International League for the Protection of Horses web site)
www.equiworld.net
(a wide range of international horse and pony information)
www.horselink.co.uk
(links for the top horse and pony care and riding web sites)

Kingfisher would like to thank:
Everybody at **The Talland School of Equitation**, especially the Hutton family and Patricia Curtis.
Everybody at **Hartpury College Equestrian Centre**, especially Margaret Linington-Payne.
Ros Sheppard, Western riding consultant.
Models: Tom Alexander, Anna Bird, Blake Christian, Emily Coles, Patricia Curtis, Wesley Davis, Sam Drinkwater, Amelia Ebanks, Naomi Ebanks, Helen Grundy, Sarah Grundy, Charlie Hutton, Pippa Hutton, Hannah James, Olivia Kuropatwa, Sophie Kuropatwa, Margaret Linington-Payne, Rhiannon Linington-Payne, Ella McEwan, Thomas McEwan, Charlotte Nagle, Gemma Oakley, Camilla Tracey, Sawako Yoshii.